WHERE

on

EARTH?

# NORTH AMERICA

By Shalini Vallepur

Designed by Brandon Mattless

Words that look like **this** can be found in the glossary on page 24.

## BookLife
## PUBLISHING

©2021
BookLife Publishing Ltd.
King's Lynn
Norfolk PE30 4LS

ISBN: 978-1-83927-201-1

**Written by:**
Shalini Vallepur

**Edited by:**
William Anthony

**Designed by:**
Brandon Mattless

# CONTENTS

# WHAT IS A CONTINENT?

A continent is a large area of land. There are seven continents on Earth. The continents are surrounded by five oceans.

North America

Arctic Ocean

Europe

Asia

Atlantic Ocean

South America

Africa

Pacific Ocean

Indian Ocean

Antarctica

Australia

Southern Ocean

N
W
S

Earth's **population** lives on the seven continents. Each continent has different types of weather and **landscape**, as well as different **cultures**.

Let's learn about North America!

# WELCOME TO NORTH AMERICA!

Where on Earth is North America? North America is a continent that is north of South America. It is also joined to South America. North and South America are surrounded by three different oceans.

Arctic Ocean

Pacific Ocean

Atl Oc

Beach in Roatán, Honduras

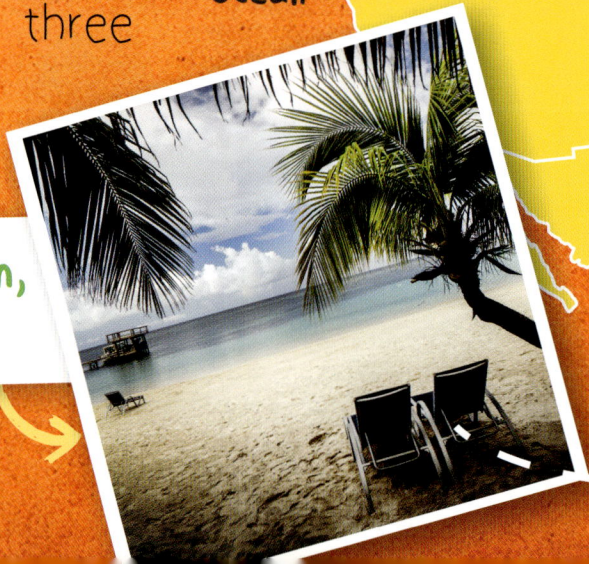

The **climate** across North America is very different. Some parts of northern Canada have a very cold climate, whereas the islands in the Caribbean have a warm, **tropical** climate.

Snowy Canada

Sunny Mexico

Winter in Canada is very different to winter in Mexico.

# Fact File:
# MEXICO

Mexico is in a part of North America called Central America. Mexico's landscape has volcanoes, **canyons** and jungles.

Mexico

Mexico City

Gulf of Mexico

Tulum National Park, Mexico

Pacific Ocean

Most Mexicans live in cities, while some live in the countryside. Many farmers live in the countryside.

Mexican city

Mexican farm

## Fact File:

**Population:**
Around 127 million

**Biggest city:**
Mexico City
(around 12 million people)

**Tallest mountain:**
Pico de Orizaba
(5,636 metres)

# NORTH AMERICAN ANIMALS

There are many
different types
of animal in North
America. Many are
**adapted** to live there.

Polar bears are large
bears that live in
snowy north Canada.
Their thick fur keeps
them warm in the snow.

Polar bear

Raccoons can be found all over North America. They can live in lots of different climates and areas. Some raccoons live in cities, although they can be dangerous to people.

Raccoon

# Fact File:
# UNITED STATES

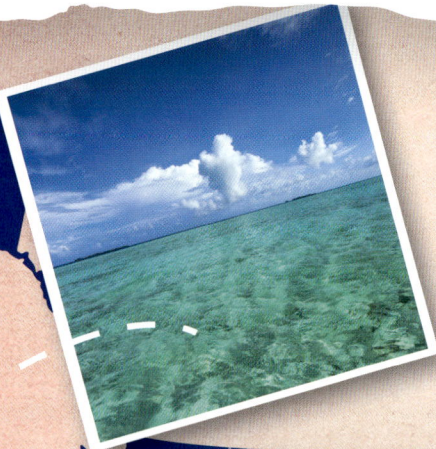

The US is made up of 50 **states**. Lots of people from all over the world live in the US.

Washington, DC

Pacific Ocean

US

Atlantic Ocean

There are lots of different landscapes in the US. The Great Basin desert is the largest desert. There are also mountains, forests and plains in the US.

The Great Basin desert

The Rocky Mountains

## Fact File:

**Population:**
Around 330 million

**Biggest city:**
New York
(over 8 million people)

**Tallest mountain:**
Mount Denali
(6,193 metres)

# PLANTS and TREES

Maple trees can be found in the US and Canada. People collect the **sap** from inside the tree and turn it into syrup to be eaten.

Collecting sap

Many tropical flowers grow in the warmer climate of the Caribbean.

Bougainvillea

Brightly coloured bougainvillea can be found in Barbados.

Golden chalice vine

The golden chalice vine grows in Cuba and Jamaica.

19

# Fact File:
# COSTA RICA

Costa Rica

San José

Costa Rica is in Central America. Costa Rica's landscape includes volcanoes, beaches and **cloud forests**.

Caribbean Sea

Pacific Ocean

Puerto Viejo, Costa Rica

There are **rainforests** in Costa Rica that are home to many different types of animal.

Cloud forest

The glass frog lives in a rainforest in Costa Rica.

## Fact File:

**Population:**
Around 5 million

**Biggest city:**
San José
(over 330,000 people)

**Tallest mountain:**
Cerro Chirripo Grande
(3,820 metres)

# NORTH AMERICAN FOOD

There are millions of people in North America and there are many delicious dishes!

Jerk chicken is a spicy chicken dish from Jamaica.

Elote is a street corn dish cooked in Mexico.

**Plantain** slices are cooked with sugar in this sweet dish from the Caribbean.

Whoopie pies are two soft cookies or cake with creamy filling from the US.

23

# GLOSSARY

| | |
|---|---|
| adapted | changed over time to suit the environment |
| canyons | large valleys with steep sides and a river flowing through |
| climate | the common weather in a certain place |
| cloud forests | forests that get a lot of rain and have clouds in the treetops |
| cultures | the traditions, ideas and ways of life of groups of people |
| landscape | how the land is laid out |
| plantain | a type of banana used for cooking |
| population | the number of people living in a certain area, such as a city or country |
| rainforests | forests that get a lot of rainfall |
| sap | a liquid inside plants that helps plants grow |
| states | areas of land that have their own leaders and make up a country |
| tropical | a hot and humid area |

# INDEX